Contents

The Stables
Ware
Herts
SG12 8LX

Printed in the UK

First Printing 2012

ISBN: 978-1-4716-7799-1

Towards a Messianic Jewish Theology of Reconciliation: The Strategic Engagement of Messianic Jewish Discourse in the Israeli-Palestinian Conflict

Abstract

Messianic Jews can play a significant part as peacemakers in the Israeli-Palestinian conflict. A theology and praxis of reconciliation is needed to address its political, social psychological and theological dimensions. Previous studies of Messianic Jewish approaches to the conflict are noted, and the method of Critical Political Discourse analysis is proposed to strategically engage Messianic Jewish theological discourse with the discourses of other conflict partners in a number of overlapping conflicts. Recent discussions of Palestinian and Israeli strategic proposals for conflict resolution provide a context in which a survey of Messianic Jewish understandings of the present conflict, proposals to end it, and the contribution Messianic Jews can make are analysed and evaluated. Concluding proposals for the development of a Messianic Jewish theology of reconciliation include the need for hope and the development of intra-group discourse that can engage strategically with other conflict partners.

1. Introduction - What is a Messianic Jewish Theology of Reconciliation?

It is the conviction of this writer that Messianic Jews are called to play a significant part in conflict resolution and reconciliation in the Israeli-Palestinian conflict. The purpose of this paper is to develop a Messianic Jewish theological discourse that can strategically engage with that of its Palestinian Christian partners in the search for peace.[1]

Messianic Jews (Jewish believers in Jesus/Yeshua) are a small minority group within both Church and Israel, yet their existence speaks of the reconciling love of the Messiah in uniting Israel and the nations in the Body of Christ.[2] They are called to speak prophetically and evangelistically to their people Israel and to the nations, reminding them of God's faithfulness to his people, his sending of his son Yeshua as Saviour and Messiah, and calling them to repentance and faith. As a prophetic sign of God's future restoration of Israel they are called to demonstrate the reconciling love of Messiah, and live out the

---

[1] I am most grateful for the assistance of many in preparing this paper. Needless to say, I alone am responsible for the views expressed and errors contained. The positions put forward are my own personal opinions, and not representative of those of any other individuals, groups or organizations within the Messianic movement.

[2] Richard S. Harvey, *Mapping Messianic Jewish Theology: A Constructive Approach* (Carlisle: Paternoster/Colorado Springs: Authentic Media, 2009), 1.

message of peace, justice and reconciliation that can transform lives and societies, and bring to an end the violent, intractable conflict that we are here to discuss. This paper will endeavour to set the context for a Messianic Jewish Theology and Practice of Reconciliation, and make some proposals for its development.

A Messianic Jewish Theology of Reconciliation (MJTOR) develops practical theological resources for Messianic Jews to contribute to the search for a just and sustainable peace. Messianic Jewish Theology affirms the ongoing election of Israel and the continuing validity of the promises of the Land as part of the Covenant promises to the Jewish people, which are now renewed and expanded in the Messiah.[3] It also recognises that Israel, despite her present state of unbelief, is called to play her full and ongoing part in God's mission to all nations and to his Creation, the *Missio Dei.* Israel is called to be a light to the nations and a model of social justice, which includes ethical righteousness, political peace, and proclamation of salvation through the death and resurrection of Yeshua.[4] Messianic Jews are called as members of the body of Messiah to be reconciled and united with their Palestinian brothers and sisters, to share their concerns and to pray and work towards the ending of an intractable conflict of 100 years. They are also called to stand alongside their people, supporting and where necessary fighting for their security and existence.

i. Previous studies

Whilst Messianic Jews have contributed to discussions with Palestinian Christians, few have proposed a program for reconciliation. They participate in organisations such as *Musalaha*, contribute to conferences such as "Christ at the Checkpoint" and books such as *Jerusalem and the Purposes of God, The Bible and the Land* and more recently, *The Land Cries Out.*[5] They share joint platforms with Palestinian Christians and participate in some of the many

---

[3] Harvey, *Mapping Messianic Jewish Theology,* 262-277.

[4] Christopher J. H. Wright, *The Mission of God: Unlocking the Bible's Grand Narrative* (Downer's Wood: IVP, 2006), 23. I go somewhat beyond Wright's own view of the ongoing particularity of Israel (the Jewish people) here, but am grateful for the paradigmatic framework he provides. I am also advocating an understanding of the calling and mission of Israel (the Jewish people) that is not held by all streams within the Messianic Jewish movement. See Harvey, *Mapping Messianic Jewish Theology,* 265-277, for a typology of Messianic Jewish theologies.

[5] Peter W. L. Walker (ed.), *Jerusalem Past and Present in the Purposes of God* (Cambridge: Tyndale House, 1992, 2nd rev. ed. 1994); Lisa Loden, Peter Walker, and Michael Wood (eds.), *The Bible and the Land: An Encounter* (Jerusalem: Musalaha, 2000); Salim J. Munayer and Lisa Loden (eds.), *The Land Cries Out: Theology of the Land in the Israeli-Palestinian Context* (USA: Cascade/Wipf and Stock, 2011).

agencies working for reconciliation.[6] But as Messianic Jews they have yet to outline a significant Theology or Praxis of Reconciliation.

In *Voices of Messianic Judaism*[7] there is no mention of the Israeli-Palestinian conflict, and only the briefest mention of the land, in the two chapters on *Aliyah*. David Stern encourages Messianic Jews to go to live in Israel, and Murray Silberling asks them to be prayerful about where God would have them be.[8] No consideration is given to the conflict, its background, or the possible roles and involvement of Messianic Jews. In my survey of the emerging theology of Messianic Judaism, I devoted a chapter to Messianic Jewish eschatology and the future of Israel, but there was only brief consideration of how Messianic Jews view the present conflict.[9] It was noted that a "bridging narrative" for a Messianic Jewish engagement with Palestinian Christians was needed, and a call for the development of a MJTOR which this paper begins to address.[10] In *The Land Cries Out* several essays by Messianic Jews are included, of which two discuss the theology of reconciliation.[11] There has been no survey of Messianic Jewish views on the Peace Process since Walter Riggans' "The Handshake".[12] Bødil Skjott surveyed Messianic Jewish views on the Land, but did not ask questions about the Israeli-Palestinian conflict directly.[13] Tsvi Sadan reviews issues discussed at previous "Christ at the Checkpoint" conferences.[14] Judith Rood presents a sustained Messianic Jewish reflection on the competing Israeli and Palestinian narratives in "Between Promise and Fulfilment: *Shoah/Nakbah* Offerings of Memory and Histories of Catastrophe".[15]

---

[6] "Israeli and Palestinian Peace-Building and Nonviolence Organizations" in *Just Vision* (Brooklyn: Encounter Point, no date) accessed January 2012 at www.justvision.org.

[7] Dan Cohn-Sherbok, ed., *Voices of Messianic Judaism: Confronting Critical Issues Facing a Maturing Movement* (USA: Lederer, 2001).

[8] Murray Silberling, "Messianic Judaism's Role in the Diaspora" and David Stern, "Messianic Jews Should Make Aliyah" in Dan Cohn-Sherbok (ed.), *Voices of Messianic Judaism,* pp. 185-192; 193-202.

[9] Harvey, *Mapping Messianic Jewish Theology,* 223-261, 264.

[10] Richard Harvey, "The Need for a Bridging Narrative" in Concordis International, *British Churches and the Israeli-Palestinian Conflict* (Concordis Papers VIII. Cambridge: Concordis International, 2010), 10-11.

[11] Salim Munayer and Lisa Loden (eds.), *The Land Cries Out: Theology of the Land in the Israeli-Palestinian Context* (USA: Cascade/Wipf and Stock, 2011).

[12] Walter Riggans, "The Messianic Jewish Community and the Handshake," *Anvil* 11.2 (1994): 145-156.

[13] Bødil Skjott, 'Messianic Believers and the Land of Israel – a Survey,' *Mishkan* 26, no. 1 (1997): 72-81.

[14] Tsvi Sadan,"Christ at the Checkpoint - and Now the Movie," *Kivun* 71(Hebrew), (Jerusalem, June-July 2010), 17-18; "The Land He has given to the children of men – except the Zionists" in *Kivun* 70 (Hebrew), (April-May 2010), 7-8.

[15] Judith Mendelsohn Rood in Margaret Hogan, ed. *What We Choose to Remember Anthology,* Garaventa Center: University of Portland, 2011 (forthcoming).

So one is left with three possible explanations for this lack of material. Either the matter is not one on which Messianic Jews have an interest or opinion, or the majority of Messianic Jews have the same view, a strong political support for Israel often based on a particular eschatology and hermeneutic of scripture. Or, as this writer has recently experienced personally in the controversy leading up to his attendance at this conference, the issue is so contentious that it cannot be properly addressed.

Whilst discussion of the Israeli-Palestinian conflict is as frequent and vocal amongst Messianic Jews as it is in the Jewish and Christian communities, the political discourse of Messianic Jews has yet to emerge from within the larger Israeli and Christian Zionist discourses in which it is situated. Just as the issue opens up cracks that show deep and complex divisions within Israeli society and Jewish communities worldwide, so the discussion of reconciliation opens up fissures within the Messianic movement, in what is also a divisive and potentially explosive way, with little clear direction set or benefit derrived.

ii. Method and Approach

Robert Schreiter notes that it is not possible to speak of one unique form of reconciliation as if *the* strategy of reconciliation exists.[16] No definitive and comprehensive study of the subject had emerged, and reconciliation needs to be worked out differently in each social and political context. Defining the meaning of reconciliation in a given context "is an important part of the reconciliation process itself". Schreiter states that this requires some measure of agreement on:

1. What and who need reconciliation
2. What will be the efficacious means for bringing that about
3. What the final state of reconciliation will look like.[17]

The parties needing reconciliation are the two sides of the Israeli-Palestinian conflict, with a particular emphasis on Messianic Jews and Palestinian Christians, but seen in the context of several other conflict systems in which they are located. The achievement of reconciliation goes beyond a just and sustainable peace at the political level. It requires a move from conflict management and conflict resolution into transformation of individuals and societies that is realised in social, psychological and spiritual dimensions.

In his introduction to *From Conflict Resolution to Reconciliation* Yaacov Bar-Siman-Tov, Professor of International Relations at the Hebrew University, poses the following questions:

---

[16] Robert J. Schreiter, *The Ministry of Reconciliation: Spirituality and Strategies* (Maryknoll: Orbis Books, 1998), 105.
[17] Schreiter, *The Ministry of Reconciliation,* 106.

1. What is the meaning and nature of reconciliation? What are its main characteristics? How can we differentiate reconciliation from stable peace? What are its major dimensions?
2. Why is reconciliation so difficult for former enemies? What kinds of conflicts require reconciliation?
3. What are the differences between reconciliation as an outcome and as a process? What are the necessary, sufficient and favourable conditions for reconciliation? What methods and techniques should be used in a reconciliation process?
4. What are the structural and psychological barriers to reconciliation? How can they be overcome?[18]

The scope of the present paper is more limited, and is not able to address all these questions. It is to explore the context and present state of a Messianic Jewish Theology and Practice of Reconciliation, and make some modest proposals as to how this will be developed. In accordance with the method of "Constructive Theology" which I have adopted previously for the study of Messianic Judaism and its theology, I aim to describe and construct a path through the terrain, identifying the key concerns and issues, and pointing to ways forward.[19] However, it will be helpful to briefly review some contemporary understandings of the concept of "Reconciliation" in political and social studies.

Daniel Bar Tal and Gemma Bennink propose that it is the "process of reconciliation itself that builds stable peace".

> Reconciliation goes beyond the agenda of formal conflict resolution to changing the motivations, goals, beliefs, attitudes and emotions of the great majority of the society members regarding the conflict, the nature of the relationships between the parties, and the parties themselves. These changes take shape via the reconciliation process, promote the peace as a new form of intergroup relations, and serve as stable foundations for cooperative and friendly acts that symbolize these relations.[20]

According to Bar Tal and Bennink,

> Reconciliation is required when the societies involved in a conflict evolve widely shared beliefs, attitude, motivations and emotions that

---

[18] Bar-Siman-Tov, Yaacov (ed.), "Introduction: Why Reconciliation?" in *From Conflict Resolution to Reconciliation* (Oxford: OUP, 2004), 3-9, 6.
[19] Harvey, *Mapping Messianic Jewish Theology,* 7-8.
[20] Daniel Bar-Tal and Gemma H. Bennink, "The Nature of Reconciliation as an Outcome and as a Process" in *From Conflict Resolution to Reconciliation,* ed. Yaacov Bar-Siman-Tov (Oxford: OUP, 2004), 11-38, 12.

> support adherence to the conflictive goals, maintain the conflict, delegitimize the opponent, and thus negate the possibility of peaceful resolution and prevent the development of peaceful relations.[21]

Reconciliation on a political level must be accompanied by psychological changes, which are the necessary basis for stable and lasting peace:

> The essence of reconciliation is a psychological process, which consists of changes of the motivations, goals, beliefs, attitudes, and emotions of the majority of society members.[22]

Lederach focuses mainly on intra-social reconciliation, focusing on four elements:

> *Truth* – which requires open expression of the past; *mercy,* which requires forgiveness to enable new relations; *justice*, which requires restitution and social restructuring; and *peace,* which entails a common future, wellbeing, and security for all the parties.[23]

Reconciliation according to the intra-societal view consists of four elements:

> (a) resolution of the conflict, which satisfies the parties' fundamental needs and fulfils their national aspirations;
> (b) mutual acceptance and respect for the other group's life and welfare;
> (c) development of a sense of security and dignity for each group;
> (d) establishment of patterns of cooperative interaction in different spheres; and
> (e) the institutionalization of conflict resolution mechanisms.[24]

Only with such psycho-social transformation can a lasting peace be achieved and maintained, so that:

> Stable and lasting peace is characterised by mutual recognition and acceptance, invested interests and goals in developing peaceful relations as well as fully normalised, cooperative political, economic, and cultural relations based on equality and justice, nonviolence, mutual trust, positive attitudes, and sensitivity and consideration for the other party's needs and interests.[25]

---

[21] Bar-Tal and Bennink, "The Nature of Reconciliation", 13.
[22] Bar-Tal and Bennink, "The Nature of Reconciliation", 17.
[23] Lederach 1997, summarized in Bar-Tal and Bennink, "The Nature of Reconciliation" 20.
[24] Bar-Tal and Bennink, "The Nature of Reconciliation", 20.
[25] Bar-Tal and Bennink, "The Nature of Reconciliation", 15.

With reconciliation as both a process and an outcome, our starting point in the process is to attempt conflict resolution at the level of the Strategic Engagement of Discourses. This paper will apply Oliver Ramsbotham's model of critical political discourse analysis to the Israeli-Palestinian conflict.[26] Working within the academic field of Peace Studies and Conflict Resolution, he proposes an approach to violent and intractable conflict through the Strategic Engagement of Discourses (SED) as a means of managing conflict and transforming it. In order to apply this approach we will first locate the Israeli-Palestinian conflict as one of a series of 'conflict systems' nested within others. We will then identify the additional conflict systems in which Messianic Jews, because of their special calling, role and context, find themselves. The results of a survey of Messianic Jewish views on the Israeli-Palestinian conflict will then be analysed and discussed as evidence of the present state of Messianic Jewish discourse. In light of these findings the elements necessary for building a peace-making infrastructure, using John Paul Lederach's work on Peace-Building and Robert Schreiter's work on reconciliation, will be proposed.[27] The conclusion will present a call for further action.

iii. Limitations

My own role as reflective practitioner not living in the region or experiencing the immediate conflict limits my contribution to this topic. I am at best a 3rd party participant coming alongside the protagonists in the Israeli-Palestinian conflict. However I come as one who is deeply situated within the theological discourses within both Church and Israel on the nature of the reconciling love of Jesus (Yeshua) the Messiah, and the ongoing election of Israel. My own background is that although I am not a "Christian Zionist", I was a Zionist before I became a Christian, and still consider myself to be one. I was always reminded that the doctor who delivered me had fought in the 1948 War of Independence. I was born in 1956, the year of the Suez crisis. I remember my family volunteering in the 1967 Six Day War. My first visit to Israel was in 1974, just after the Yom Kippur War. I have always wanted, and pray that God will allow, despite my attendance at this conference, to live in the Land. I am not a "Christian Zionist" because I do not hold to a particular Dispensationalist hermeneutic or eschatology wedded to a right-wing political position on Israeli-Palestinian conflict. But I would still call myself a Zionist, or perhaps a "post-Zionist". I prefer the term "Messianic Jew", rather than Christian because of its negative connotations the word "Christian" has for my people. But providing it is rightly understood as meaning 'a disciple of Yeshua' I am willing to be called a Christian. I come to the study of Messianic Jewish Theology

---

[26] Oliver Ramsbotham, *Transforming Violent Conflict: Radical Disagreement, Dialogue and Survival* (London and New York: Routledge, 2010).
[27] John Paul Lederach, *Building Peace – Sustainable Reconciliation in Divided Societies* (Tokyo: United Nations University Press, 1997). Robert J. Schreiter, *The Ministry of Reconciliation: Spirituality and Strategies* (Maryknoll: Orbis, 1998).

(MJT) as a Messianic Jew from the United Kingdom, wanting to apply both academic method and personal faith commitment to the search for peace, justice and reconciliation. My presence and presentation here offers a small contribution to the resolution of this terrible ongoing conflict.

2. Messianic Jews and Conflict Systems

Messianic Jews are caught up in a conflict system made up of some ten related and overlapping "conflict complexes" or "formations". The Israeli-Palestinian conflict is situated within the wider conflict between Israel and her Arab neighbours. This includes unresolved conflicts with Syria and Lebanon. The Arab-Israeli conflict formation is set within the wider Middle East conflict area that includes Iran and Turkey. The Middle East conflict is part of the global conflict between radical Islam and conservative Jewish and Christian groups, and the geo-political interests of the United States, Western Europe and the other global powers.[28]

In addition to these local, regional and global conflict systems, Messianic Jews are involved in other ideological and theological levels of conflict within the Body of Christ, all of which require reconciliation. These further seven levels of conflict arise at the theological, group and inter-personal level.

1. Messianic Jews need to be reconciled to their Palestinian brothers and sisters in Christ.
2. They need to be reconciled to Arab Christians in general.
3. Messianic Jews need to be reconciled with Christian Zionists, who challenge the role of Messianic Jews in Evangelism and whose theological and political agenda they often do not fit.[29]
4. Messianic Jews need to be reconciled to a wider Church that is often supersessionist in its theology, and contains anti-Judaism. [30]
5. Messianic Jews need to be reconciled with Christian Anti-Zionists and Anti-Christian Zionists.[31] Here the radical disagreement is strongest, and these are the two groups to which many at this conference belong!

---

[28] Ramsbotham, 166.

[29] Baruch Maoz. "The Christian Embassy in Jerusalem" in Mishkan (Issue 12) on *Christian Zionism* (UCCI/Caspari Centre, Jerusalem, 1990) and the collection of articles in Mishkan (Issue 55) on *Israel, the Land, and Christian Zionism* (ed. Kai Kjær-Hansen) (UCCI/Caspari Centre: Jerusalem, 2008); Richard S. Harvey, "Implicit 'Universalism' in Some Christian Zionism and Messianic Judaism" in *Jesus, Salvation and the Jewish People: The Uniqueness of Jesus and Jewish Evangelism*, ed. David Parker (UK: Paternoster, 2011).

[30] R. Kendall Soulen, *The God of Israel and Christian Theology* (Minneapolis: Fortress Press, 1999). It is not the major focus of this paper to address the issue of supersessionism, but it is this writer's belief that the supposed dualism between "Covenant" and "Restoration" theologies is largely a result of the failure of Christian theology to address this issue.

[31] I am making a distinction here and throughout between Christians who oppose Zionism as the Jewish and Israeli political ideology and project ("Christian Anti-Zionism") and

6. Messianic Jews also find themselves in conflict with the Jewish community, as aspects of Judaism (religion), Jewishness (culture and ethnicity) and Israeli identity (civil, political and nationality) also raise profound challenges to them as believers in Yeshua.[32]
7. Finally, amongst themselves, there is intra-group conflict on these issues.

One way to understand the nature of such conflicts and respond to them is to analyse the discourses of disagreement within each conflict, and engage them strategically.

3. Critical Political Discourse Analysis of Intractable Conflict

Intractable conflicts are the most serious political conflicts where settlement and transformation fail – or are yet to succeed. They are violent, persistent and destructive, affecting families, society and nations down through the generations.[33] They are characterised by violence and hopelessness. *Radical disagreements* are the chief linguistic manifestation of intractable conflicts, intersecting the spheres of human difference, human discourse and human conflict.[34]

> Wars of words are propaganda battles and contests for media control. But at a deeper level, they are also conflicts of belief. They are clashes of perspective, horizons and visual fields. I call them radical disagreements. Linguistic intractability lies at the heart of the communicative aspect of intractable conflict in general, which is defined here as conflict that has so far defied all attempts at conflict resolution and conflict transformation.[35]

In the Israeli-Palestinian conflict the Israeli security discourse, "the Palestinian liberation discourse and the international (UN) peace-making and state-building discourses (among others) all struggle for supremacy".[36] Each party tries to impose its own language, wanting to provide the "lens through which

---

Christians who oppose "Christian Zionism" which I define more narrowly as those employing a Dispensational Premillennialist hermeneutic wedded to a particular political support and engagement with right wing Israeli political positions ("Anti-Christian Zionism"). There is overlap between the two. Historic Premillennial and Amillennialist support for the Zionist project, which was originally advocated by several early "restorationists" such as Shaftesbury and Wilberforce, is not directly equivalent to the narrower form of Christian Zionism. See Paul Charles Merkely, *Christian Attitudes Towards the State of Israel* (McGill-Queen's University Press, 2001).

32 Richard Harvey, "What Shapes Jewish Identity" in *Sixth International Conference 1999 Conference Booklet* (Lausanne Consultation on Jewish Evangelism, August 13, 1999), 72-85.

33 Ramsbotham, *Transforming Violent Conflict,* 1.

34 Ramsbotham, 2010:15.

35 Ramsbotham, 2011:57.

36 Ramsbotham, 2010:17.

the conflict is viewed". Within each conflict system there may be a power imbalance, or asymmetry. The conflict parties and sub-groups within each party may find themselves alternating in their relative power and influence, and the ability to impose their own discourse.

Critical political discourse analysis is an interdisciplinary approach to the study of such disagreements, that views language as a "form of social practice and focuses on the ways social and political domination are said to be visible in text and talk".

> Critical-political discourse analysis deals especially with the reproduction of political *power, power abuse* or *domination* through political discourse, including the various forms of resistance or counter-power against such forms of discursive dominance. In particular such an analysis deals with the discursive conditions and consequences of social and political *inequality* that results from such domination.[37]

From a theological perspective, the critical analysis of radical disagreement is a useful tool, as the language used to describe conflict is fraught not only with theological issues, but is used to formulate arguments that justify ideology and power interests. For theologians it is important to engage with the issues through the study of discourse rather than employ a historical, political, social-psychological or method, as many of the arguments put forward, especially by those Christians who support the claims of one side or the other, are stated in theological as well as political terms.[38] For Messianic Jews, as for Palestinian Christians, it is important to understand the social and political dynamics inherent in the language they use, and that used by others.

Critical discourse analysis of radical disagreement can harness such disagreements into what Ramsbotham calls the "Strategic Engagement of Discourses" (SED). Even where the conflict partners are in radical disagreement with one another, the dynamic of their disagreement may be amenable through the influence of other discourse partners to a more strategic engagement of discourse that might lead to dialogue. This may reduce the preference for the option of violence and begin to facilitate a more pro-active stance on negotiation, conflict management and resolution, and prepare for peace.

---

[37] Teun A. van Dijk, "What is political discourse analysis?" (Key-note address, Congress Political Linguistics. Antwerp, 7-9 -December 1995) in Jan Blommaert and Chris Bulcaen (Eds.), *Political Linguistics* (Amsterdam: Benjamins, 1997), 11-52, 1.

[38] For discussion of Critical Discourse Analysis and Political Theology, see Clayton Crockett, *Radical Political Theology: Religion and Politics after Liberalism* (USA, Columbia University Press, 2011), Ch. 1, "The Parallax of Religion: Theology and Ideology", pp.26-42. For the relationship between Theology and the Social Sciences, see Kathryn Tanner, *Theories of Culture: A New Agenda for Theology (Guides to Theological Enquiry),* (USA: Augsburg/Fortress, 1997).

There needs to be three stages of engagement. Before *dialogue for mutual understanding* is possible, *dialogue for strategic engagement* must occur, which means there will be "not less radical disagreement but more". This can enable the *strategic engagement of discourses* (SED). There are six engagements of discourse that must take place in each conflict system, in a hexagon of radical disagreement (figure 1, below[39]). The "moderates" and "extremists" have to engage with each other both within and across the conflict parties.[40]

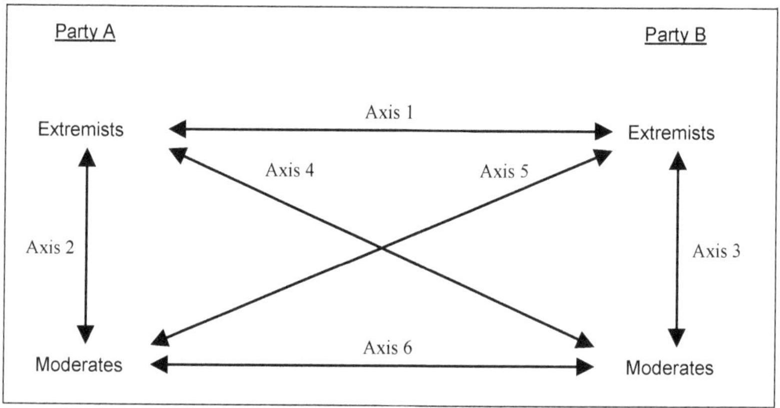

Figure 1. The hexagon of radical disagreement (Ramsbotham, 2010: 192)

Within each party to the conflict there needs to be an internal discussion, the 'intra-party strategic engagement of discourses' (Level 1). This requires strategic thinking within the group when its desire to overcome its internal divisions which prevent it from acting in a united way becomes "strong enough to counteract the influence of would-be internal hegemons wanting to impose their own exclusive discourses".[41]

> The motive for pursuing intra-party strategic discursive engagement of this kind is not to promote mutual understanding with the enemy. On the contrary, it is the fear that internal weakness will jeopardize the external national struggle.[42]

---

[39] Ramsbotham, 2010:192.

[40] I am using the terms "moderate" and "extreme" throughout according to Ramsbotham's usage (*Transforming Violent Conflict,* 193): "The terms 'extremist' and 'moderate' will vary across different issues and are themselves contested". They are a means of mapping the spectrum of discourses from the least to the most intractable, rather than implying a moral judgment in the light of the writer's own personal views.

[41] Ramsbotham, 2010:168.

[42] Ibid.

The next of engagement of strategic discourses is inter-party (Level 2), where the strategic thinking within the group engages with the strategic thinking of the other conflict party. In asymmetric conflicts, where the balance of power is unequal,

> [I]t is the challenging discourse (the discourse of the weaker party – the challenger) that has a greater incentive to promote strategic engagement, while the hegemonic discourse (the discourse of the more powerful party – the possessor) has a greater interest in ignoring it or suppressing it. Either way, where there is strategic engagement, each party's main aim is, once again, not to understand the other, but to win.[43]

The final level of Strategic Engagement of Discourses (Level 3) involves third parties appealed to by the conflict parties, such as other nations, NGOs, peacemakers, and observers.

> Of particular interest here is the engagement of the discourses of those third parties, who see themselves, or claim to be, disinterested peacemakers. These are now recognised as yet further discourses struggling to occupy the whole of the discursive space and to dictate the course of unfolding events.[44]

For Messianic Jews the challenge is to situate their own strategic discourse for peace and reconciliation within the context of the emerging engagement of strategic discourses of the Israeli and Palestinian conflict partners so that they can then engage with their Palestinian Christian partners.[45] In order to do this we will survey the strategic thinking within the Israeli and Palestinian groups, before assessing the Messianic Jewish contribution.

Messianic Jews identify primarily with the concerns of Israel and the Jewish people. In order to contribute to the process of reconciliation, they need to be aware of the strategic thinking that is taking place within Israeli and Palestinian discourses, and respond to that, with their own biblical reflections, theological development, and practical engagement. We will consider Messianic Jewish views on the peace-process below, but first consideration will be given to recent Israeli and Palestinian strategic discussions on options for peace.[46]

---

[43] Ramsbotham, 2010:168.
[44] Ramsbotham, 2010:168-9.
[45] It is beyond the purpose of this paper to identify and describe the different Palestinian Christian positions, which I expect will be brought out by other papers at this conference.
[46] For what follows here see Ramsbotham 2010:165-204, "Praxis: Managing Agonistic Discourse"; Oliver Ramsbotham, "Radical Disagreement and Systemic Conflict Transformation" in D. Körppen, N. Ropers and Hans J. Gießmann (eds.), *The Non-Linearity of*

4. Palestinian Intra-Group Discourse

In 2006-9 the Oxford Research Group facilitated separate Palestinian and Israeli meetings to formulate strategic options for peace, as "few Israelis or Palestinians at the time at political level were interested in dialogue for mutual understanding".[47] On the Palestinian side, an inclusive strategy group of 40 met several times to produce *Regaining the Initiative: Palestinian Strategic Options to End Israeli Occupation*,[48] which made detailed proposals for future peace. Its Executive Summary noted the present lack of options for the Peace Process, and considered eight strategic options. It noted the acceptable and unacceptable options for the Palestinians:

> Four scenarios acceptable to many or most Palestinians are:
>
> (1) A fully sovereign Palestinian state on the 1967 borders with Jerusalem as its capital, and a just settlement that fulfills the Palestinian refugees' right to return and compensation.
> (2) A single bi-national state for Israelis and Palestinians.
> (3) A single democratic state in which all citizens are treated equally before the law.
> (4) A confederation between Jordan and an independent Palestinian state.
>
> Scenarios not acceptable to Palestinians are:
>
> (5) Continuation of the status quo, with open-ended and intermittent negotiations providing cover for continuing Israeli settlement on Palestinian land and the consolidation of the occupation.
> (6) A Palestinian state with temporary borders and limited sovereignty, permanently under the effective control of Israel.
> (7) Unilateral separation by Israel with imposed borders and restrictions on the movement of Palestinians.

Peace Processes – Theory and Practice of Systemic Conflict Transformation (Opladen/Farmington Hills: Barbara Budrich Verlag, 2011); www. berghof-peacesupport.org/books/sct_book_2011_Ramsbotham.pdf (accessed January 2011); Ofer Zalzberg, *EU Partnership for Peace – Israeli Track* (Oxford Research Group, Jerusalem, 22 April 2009). Available at www. kms1.isn.ethz.ch/serviceengine/Files/.../10-04+**EU**-PfP-Israel.pdf (accessed January 2011).

[47] Ramsbotham, 2011: 66.

[48] The Palestine Strategy Group, "Towards New Strategies for Palestinian National Liberation", available at http://www.palestinestrategygroup.ps/Towards_New_Strategies_For_Palestinian_National_Liberation_FINAL_8-2011_(English).pdf. "The Palestine Strategy Group (PSG) is an open and inclusive forum for strategic discussion in which Palestinians from across the social and political spectrum conduct strategic analysis of the environment of the conflict with Israel in order to strengthen and guide the Palestinian national project for liberation and independence."

(8) Any notions involving the absorption of Gaza by Egypt and the West Bank by Jordan, or other comparable arrangements.[49]

For the Palestinian group a strategic aim was to exclude the unacceptable scenarios because the Israeli side might believe these are preferable to agreeing a settlement and are permanently available, thus removing the need for serious negotiations.

5. Israeli Intra-Group Discourse

The parallel Israeli group also represented a wide variety of constituencies within Israeli society. It consisted of emerging leaders from across the spectrum of political opinion across religious, secular, academic, military, business, social and political life.[50] The proposals that the group developed were not so much linked to the problems of Gaza and the West Bank, but were more related to what the future state would look like, and the distinction between Jewishness (cultural Jewish identity), Zionism (national Jewish identity) and Judaism (religious Jewish identity). [51] The social fragmentation of Jewish Israeli society became the main concern of the discussion. How the group defined Jewish (cultural, religious) and Israeli identity (national, diplomatic) became key concerns and make it difficult to agree on a common strategy.

> In Israel, the Jewish Israeli society is governed by the anxiety of the traumatic past of the Jewish people, and the wish for a secure existence at all costs. The deep division within the Jewish Israeli society is about how to secure itself and achieve a sustainable peace with its neighbours. This fragmentation is reflected in the divergence in priorities, values and goals and a deep mistrust among the main streams of society. It is a result both of social cleavages (religious-secular, socioeconomic left-right, Ashkenaz-Sepharad, immigrants-natives) and of the pressures caused by the Israeli-Palestinian conflict (as well as some related regional conflicts).[52]

The group did not produce strategic options, but four "future stories" based on possible scenarios, using the analogy of "homes":

#1 A Jewish Home - From the Jordan to the Mediterranean
Failure of negotiations and resulting radicalization and violence coupled with a significant demographic growth of the national religious and the ultra orthodox aggravate poverty and a mass emigration of secular

---

[49] "Towards New Strategies For Palestinian National Liberation", 2011: 12.
[50] Zalzberg, 2009:2.
[51] Zalzberg, 2009:4.
[52] Zalzberg, 1.

population overseas. A new Israeli policy based on religious-national and national-social values causes the Arabs to despair from establishing a Palestinian state and accept a limited status of individual residents –not citizens- within Israel. Militant Palestinians are dealt with severe violence.

#2 Two Homes for Two Peoples – Good Neighbours
A joint understanding among Israelis and Palestinians about the need to divide the land if one wants to avoid a bi-national state. Implementation of the two state agreement is based on an international force ensuring Israeli security in the West Bank initially. A set of domestic mutual compromises between groups in Israel is enabled and leads to closing social gaps by including Israeli-Arabs and ultra-orthodox Jews in governmental institutions and the Knesset adopting a constitution based on the declaration of independence.

#3 One Home for Two Peoples – Isra-Palestine
The US decision to abandon the Middle East leaves Israel with an unprecedented diplomatic, security and economic crisis. International pressure forces Israel to establish an Israeli- Palestinian state between the Jordan River and the Sea. The government will be composed of neutral professionals for 40 years and the IDF will be replaced by an Israeli-Palestinian army based on the Lebanese multi-ethnic model. Both the Jewish and the Palestinian societies are torn amongst themselves and those opposing the new reality actively demonstrate their feelings at times violently. Massive emigration of Jews strengthens Jewish centres in the US and Germany and only true believers (either in religious or in egalitarian-democratic beliefs) or those economically unable to move remain in the state.

#4 A Shared Home – A Jewish Home as part of a Regional Confederation.
In the context of a global economic recession the US reduces its Middle East involvement while Europe and Russia use their increased influence to run the PA as a protectorate under International (especially Arab) administration. A new international "coalition of hope" proposes a peace deal based on cooperation between religions, nations, states and businesses. Israel decides to adopt these ideas and promotes a peace initiative which includes the creation of a confederation under an international umbrella. Palestine and Jordan agree to become members of the confederation. Member states are responsible for education, culture, private law, religious services, etc. Economy, infrastructure and security are managed at the confederate level. Some Jewish settlements in Judea, Samaria and the Golan Heights remain in their place through a lease agreement while the Old City of Jerusalem is declared confederate territory. The new confederation has the opportunity to become a member state in the European Union. The Near East Market, which

includes Egypt, Syria and Lebanon, attracts massive foreign investments.[53]

Such divergent options between the two parties reveals the disjuncture between them, but also provides deeper understanding of the aims of the two sides. For the Palestinians, the strategy process enabled them to focus as a unified group on a set of strategic options in pursuit of their goals. For the Israelis, the focus was on the "tension between different kinds of Jewish sovereignty and different kinds of Jewish identity in Israel".[54]

Each scenario presented a choice of benefits and costs related to the degree of Jewish sovereignty and the type of Jewish identity that resulted.

> For example, a regional-confederal constellation secures firmly a stable situation of cultural autonomy for Jews but limits their sovereignty. Inversely, practicing Jewish sovereignty from the Jordan to the Mediterranean is arguably achievable only in the context of a religious orthodox militaristic hegemony of the Israeli-Jewish society.
> Put differently, the character of the state, and in particular the manner in which it is Jewish (culturally / nationally / religiously), was thus flagged as an intermediating factor between the internal Jewish debate on identity and the external political constraints, mostly imposed by the conflictual reality Israel faces in the Middle East.[55]

This is illustrated by the table below:

	Jewish Sovereignty	**Jewish Identity**
A Jewish Home	Nation-state (territory)	Religious Orthodox Zionist militaristic hegemony
Two Homes for Two Peoples	Nation-state (people)	Secular Zionist statist hegemony
One Home for Two Peoples	None	Communal (Jewish in private & public sphere but not state)
A Shared Home	Limited Sovereignty	An ethnic territorial group (Jewishness = cultural autonomy)

Table 1: Jewish Sovereignty and Identity (Zalzberg 2009:7)

53 Zalzberg, 6.
54 Zalzberg, 7.
55 Zalzberg, 7.

6. Messianic Jewish Intra-Group Discourse

As we note the way Palestinians and Israelis have formulated strategic options and scenarios as part of their intra-group discourse, we recognise that without such initial intra-group discussions it is not possible for them to strategically engage with "moderate" and "extreme" positions on the other side, or with third parties. How can Messianic Jews develop their own intra-group discourse in a similar way in order to engage strategically with the discourse of the other side, and with third parties? We now turn to a survey and assessment of Messianic Jewish discourse, assessing their views of the conflict and their proposals for solutions. We attempt a strategic intra-group engagement of discourse within the group in order to formulate a strategic proposals for peace and reconciliation.

Messianic Jews have yet to produce strategic options for peace, and have not yet formulated their own positions on the question, although these are the subject of heated informal debate. For the purpose of this paper a survey of their views was conducted in January 2012. Messianic leaders of congregations and other organisations were sent a questionnaire asking the following four questions:

> *1. Are you optimistic or pessimistic about the possibility of peace in the Israel-Palestine/Arab-Israeli conflict? Why?*
>
> *2. What would be your own proposals/preferred outcome be for a peace settlement in the Arab/Israeli conflict?*
>
> *3. What approach or strategy do you think Israel should adopt to achieve this?*
>
> *4. What do you think Messianic Jews can contribute to reconciliation and peace in the Arab-Israeli conflict? How can they do this?*[56]

The survey was sent by email to 80 people, with a 56% response.[57] The 45respondents are broadly representative of the Messianic movement worldwide, with 36% (16) from Israel, 31% (14) from the UK, 27% (12) from the USA and 7% (3) from other countries. The gender ratio was 78% (35) male and 22% (10) female. 12% (5) were emerging leaders, 44% (20) established and 44% (20) in senior leadership. Two Hebrew Catholic participants contributed, and a control group of interested others were invited to participate, whose responses are not included. Participants were assured that they would be treated anonymously, so are referred to numerically. What

[56] In hindsight, the questions should have retained the "Israel-Palestine" focus throughout. Only one respondent noted this, but all answered with the Israel-Palestine conflict in mind.
[57] As of February 1st 2012.

follows is a summary of the positions represented, with illustrative quotations, chosen on the basis of the originality of the formulations or their broad representation of the views of others.[58]

1. Are you optimistic or pessimistic about the possibility of peace in the Israel-Palestine/Arab-Israeli conflict? Why?

71 % (32) were pessimistic, including 7% (3) who were 'very pessimistic'. Reasons given for the pessimism include:

- An intractable conflict
    - An enormous and unbridgeable gap between the two sides
    - Irreconcilable differences in the facts and narrative about the conflict
- Hatred and prejudice towards Israel
    - The majority of Palestinians support violence
    - The danger of Islam/Hamas
    - Islamic anti-Semitism has merged with Palestinian anti-Zionism
    - Koranic injunctions to *Jihad*
    - Lack of will from the other Moslem countries to moderate their attitude to Israel.
- No political solution possible
    - The pain of compromise which neither side is willing to make
    - No Palestinian leader with whom to negotiate
    - No guarantee of security if Israel concedes territory
    - No solution to the refugee problem
    - Lack of realism by the International community in treating issues such as integrating Gaza into Egypt and the West Bank into Jordan.
- Demographic factors
    - Palestinian population increase
    - Growth of right-wing Jewish orthodoxy
- Present circumstances
    - "The Gaza withdrawal and its disastrous aftermath must make any sort of peace deal seem suspect."[59]
- Not enough desire for Peace
    - "If both sides could look at themselves first, their own failings, then I would be more optimistic"[60]
- Spiritual Issues
    - The problem is a spiritual conflict against satanic opposition
    - There will be no peace until the return of the Messiah
    - A political solution will not change the hearts of the actors[61]

---

[58] Not all respondents answered every question.

[59] Respondent no. 31.

[60] Respondent no. 38.

[61] *I am pessimistic because: 1) the conflict has grown deeper and become more exacerbated over the decades; 2) Islamic anti-Semitism is deeply merged with Palestinian anti-Zionism,*

However, 18% (8) described themselves 'realistic rather than optimistic or pessimistic'; 'very slightly optimistic'; 'a short-term pessimist with long-term optimism'; 'as a person... pessimistic, as a believer ... called to be optimistic'; 'pessimistically optimist'; 'in essence, a pessimistic optimist!'[62] 7%(3) described themselves as 'optimistic'.

---

making it difficult to imagine real, lasting peace; 3) from my understanding of Scripture, the only peace we will see before Yeshua returns will be fleeting and ultimately false, although both sides must still work towards it with sincerity. (7)
To be honest, I am quite pessimistic. It seems on both sides one step forward is always followed by 5 steps backwards. (8)
I would say "totally pessimistic" if I did not mind using an understatement in the present case. (18)
I am pessimistic about a resolution to this conflict between Palestinians and Israelis because the forces perpetuating the conflict are the radical and unilateral movements in both our nations. Peace to them (both Israeli and Palestinian sides) is equivalent to compromise of a rock-hard ideology. (19)
Apart from the work of Yeshua on individual hearts, I am not optimistic. (23)
Peace is not feasible anywhere in the near future, the reason being the Palestinian refusal to end the conflict once and for all. At the same time the present situation of no peace but no conflict can last until the parties will agree on permanent borders and a Jewish state. (34)
So why am I a pessimist? It is because, like many people today, I have lost faith in politicians and negotiators. Maybe this is a failed view of the situation. Why do I look to men to be the source of this peace? Why do I not see God as an usher of the political process? I am not sure and I am open to be challenged. All I know is that my attitude is negative towards what could be a lot of good – that's a problem. (40)
I am not optimistic that a peace treaty in the UN perspective of it would work. But I am sure that in due time the truth of Israel's calling back to the Land and the Almighty's promises to the people, will trickle in to more and more of our neighbouring Arabs and cause them to change their perspective which can bring more peace. (41)
Pessimistic, because I don't see that the Palestinians have any interest whatsoever in a two-state solution. They want a one-state solution, by which I mean that they want the state of Israel not to exist. That can't bring peace. I have reached this conclusion only after living here 32 years, during which time I moved from being in favour of working toward a two-state solution to my present position. (48)

[62] *I hope I am realistic rather than either optimistic or pessimistic. If I must describe my views according to these categories, then I am pessimistic about an immediate or short term solution to the conflict. I am, however, cautiously optimistic about a solution that could be negotiated over the long term.* (20)
I am optimistic about the possibility of peace. It seems to me that the stalemate can only endure for so long, and my impression is that a large block of moderates on both sides are increasingly eager to find a peaceful resolution and increasingly willing to engage one another in dialogue. There are several initiatives to this end that I find to be very hopeful. (33)
I also can't help but think that true peace will only come when Yeshua returns, but that does not mean that 'good people should stand by and do nothing!' So, in essence, a pessimistic, optimist! (38)
In due time the truth of Israel's calling back to the Land and the Almighty's promises to the people, will trickle in to more and more of our neighbouring Arabs and cause them to change their perspective which can bring more peace. (41)

Reasons given for optimism were:

- The great international pressure for a settlement
- The growing Israeli desire for a settlement
- The increasing number of Palestinians and Israelis demonstrating reconciliation in Christ[63]
- "God is eternally faithful and He will yet surprise us"[64]
- Long-term optimism at the return of Jesus[65]

Reflection. The general pessimism and lack of hope was most apparent, but this was not unanimous. One factor that was not mentioned was the Arab Spring. Nor did anyone mention Palestinian initiatives at Peace-Building or Reconciliation, apart from one mention of *Musalaha.*[66] The discourse of the respondents reflected the same factors found in Israeli discourse of concern for security, no workable options on the table, no discussion partners, combined with a theological perspective that rationalised the eschatological solution to the problem as the only hopeful outcome.

2. What would be your own proposals/preferred outcome be for a peace settlement in the Arab/Israeli conflict?

Most favoured some version of a two-state solution, although this was not unanimous. Proposals included:

A. One Israeli State[67]

The most optimistic scenario is for managed hostility. That's not as negative as it might sound - it's actually the situation in much of Northern Ireland today, which is seen as a success story. (46)

63 *Optimistic - I believe in the power of prayer, and of witness by Jewish Believers and Gentile Believers and in the grassroots activity which is bringing fantastic small-scale reconciliation in and beyond The Land, from a variety of community initiatives.* (1)

64 Respondent no. 25.

65 *I am optimistic, it will happen when Jesus returns. Why? Because that is what the Bible says.* (35)

I am pessimistically-optimistic. My understanding of the Bible does not allow me to see the peace between Jews and Arabs established unless God intervenes by His second coming. (39)

66 Respondent no. 1.

67 *I believe that ALL the land of Israel belongs to Israel including of course East Jerusalem and the so-called occupied territories. So to have temporary reconciliation one side has to give up on her national and religious expectations.* (39)

Palestinians who want to live under a Jewish state should be given citizenship, and ... the heartland of Israel should be annexed. I think Israel should not give in to pressure from the nations who ultimately are not looking for peace, but for another means to put down Israel and force their politics on the Israeli people. This means that Israel should in the right timing annex the Land and grant citizenship to those Palestinians who want to live in a Jewish state as law-abiding citizens. (41)

- All the Land belongs to Israel
- Build high walls around the current settlements
- Develop the Iron Dome program.
- Occupation and "managed hostility"[68]
- Develop a satisfactory narrative for the future of the settlements

B. Two State Solution[69]

- "Land for Peace"
- Jerusalem remains under Jewish control

I would like the Jewish people to have all the land that God has promised them - yes all of it! I would prefer that to happen without any loss of life. (42)
If a Palestinian state were created it would be on a trajectory towards full statehood, with its own army. The election of Hamas in Gaza shows how dangerous such a situation could become. (46)
[68] *The present situation of no peace but no conflict can last until the parties will agree on permanent borders and Jewish state.* (10)
The current approach of occupation and managed hostility seems to be the best proposal that realism allows. (46)
[69] *I believe in a 2 state solution which is no doubt only a temporal solution. There cannot be any settlement that does not recognize both the legitimate political/social aspirations of the Palestinians and the security concerns of the Israelis.* (6)
Hamas renounces its terrorism and acknowledges the rights of the Jewish state; the PA does the same; Israel examines its attitudes and treatment of the Palestinians to resolve wrongs on its own end; Jerusalem remain firmly under Jewish control as the national capital; defensible borders be agreed upon for a Palestinian state. (7)
Two-State solution with defensible borders and as much integrated commerce as possible and other initiatives (e.g., education, sports, Arts). (9)
I would be in favour of the Barak proposal that the Clinton administration (during its closing days) presented to Arafat, and which he rejected. (10)
The same as most mainstream Israeli politicians left or right: a demilitarized Palestinian state within the West Bank. Preferably for us, to keep east Jerusalem, large settlement blocs... (15)
As a temporary peace, Israel keeps the major settlements near the borders, and swaps land in lieu of this. The Arabs are given East Jerusalem as a capital but there is open passage for the city and economic unity. The refugee issue will not be settled. They will be allowed to settle in the West Bank, or other countries and some few 10,000 will come back re: family. The Arabs will not accept this. So there will be a principle of compensation and a peace without a final solution to protect the Arab negotiators. (17)
I am not against 'land for peace,' but I am against 'land for nothing' as happened with Gaza. We should work toward peace, but not be naive. (23)
A genuine two-state solution, with lots of trade and interaction between Israel and a Palestinian state, and lots of support and participation by the surrounding Arab states, would be ideal, but probably unlikely. (31)
I prefer Israel to withdraw unilaterally to the 1967 borders as a last chance to unite Jews in Israel. (34)
I would like to see a Palestinian state in the West Bank, where Jews are allowed to be full citizens. I would like to see a Jewish state in which Palestinian Arabs can thrive. I would like to see Israel defeat Hamas in Gaza, and for the UN or Egypt to take control of the Gaza strip, ensuring full rights for Palestinians. I would compensate all victims of exiles in 1948, including the Palestinian Arabs forced out of Israel, and the hundreds of thousands of Jews forced out of Muslim lands following the birth of the Jewish state. (37)

- "Normal" diplomatic and economic relationships between those states
- Regional support
- Integration of commerce, education, sports, etc.

C. One Democratic State[70]

- Equal rights for all citizens, equal representation in government, and equal access to all goods and services
- Cultural and philosophical change needed[71]

D. No Obvious Solution[72]

Reflection. The options given reflect a preference for a Two-State Solution, which overlaps with general Israeli opinion, but is in marked contrast to most Christian Zionist thinking. Also the emerging One State option is not beyond the consideration of some Messianic Jews, and is likely to become more popular with the younger generation of emerging leaders due to the emphasis on human rights.

3. What approach or strategy do you think Israel should adopt to achieve this?

a. Negotiation and willingness to compromise[73]

---

[70] *What is more important is for there to be equal opportunity for both Arab and Jew but under the State of Israel, not a two State Solution. This should somehow be encouraged and there be should be no barrier between the two.* (14)
I would prefer a one state solution with equal rights for all citizens, equal representation in government, and equal access to all goods and services. (19)
Until people are willing to deal with the underlying cultural and philosophical conflicts, the peoples will barely know how to talk to each other, let alone do business and run inter-racial administrative offices. (40)

[71] *Israel needs to culturally reorient - we are a part of the Middle East and not of Western Europe or North America. Arabic must become the second language of every Jewish Israeli.* (26)

[72] *I believe firmly in a settlement that respects both parties to the conflict, their histories, their identities and their demands for justice and security. Whether this will take the form of two states, one state, no state is less important for me. The political settlement will depend on profound social, cultural changes that must happen. Jewish Israelis are called to situate themselves firmly in the region (I believe that this means a cultural reorientation - learning Arabic, getting to know the region ...) and Palestinians and Arabs in general will need to reorient themselves to a pluralist Middle East in which Jews and Christians are a welcome presence ...* (26)
I do not know. I am just waiting for the Messiah to manage it in His way. (30)
Preach the Gospel, that is our only hope. (35)

[73] *Palestinian refugee/rights issue, which will necessarily require compromise on Israel's part.* (33)
The continued construction of settlements is an ongoing hindrance to lasting peace, and a repeated provocation to the Palestinian people. (33)

b. No negotiation with terrorists[74]

c. Stop building settlements[75]

d. Civil War if settlements dismantled[76]

e. Need for Strategic Engagement of Discourses/Bridging Narrative[77]

f. A truth and reconciliation process[78]

g. Change of Law/Constitution[79]

h. Managed hostility[80]

i. Grass-roots peace movement[81]

Reflection. Just as the variety of possible solutions differed greatly, so do the means of achieving them. Some took a hard line approach, no negotiation with terrorists, no dismantling of settlements, no territorial concessions, and no compromise. This was the discourse of 5 respondents (11%). However, 56%

---

[74] *Stand firm and wait for Palestinians to cease the rhetoric of Israel destruction.* (13) *Relying on God and not paying attention to all sorts of Western double-standard democracies. No negotiations with terrorists both Fatah and Hamas. Address Palestinian rights.* (39)

[75] *Israel should stop building any further settlements - not because I think they are illegal (that is disputable), nor because I think that any part of the world, least of all areas of millennia-long significance to Jews, should be Jew-free - but because that would take away Abbas' one excuse for not returning to the negotiating table.* (44)

[76] *Offer honourable viable alternatives for settlers along with referendum that will prove citizens' preferences on this question. Forced evacuation will lead to civil war this time.* (34)

[77] *"Facts" are useless in the real world, as there are differing narratives all offering "facts", many of which are indisputable.* (15)
For irreconcilable differences in the facts and narrative about the conflict see "From Time Immemorial: The Origins of the Arab-Jewish Conflict Over Palestine" by Joan Peters. (16)

[78] *The most important approach is to come to the negotiating table with a shared commitment to listen to the other side. This should be done on the basis of prior education and exposure to the culture, world view and mindset of the opposing side in the conflict. Following that all issues should be open for discussion and negotiation.* (20)

[79] *Fundamental to any progress toward a solution, in my understanding, is a change of basic law in Israel to enable a true democratic process to emerge. This includes a constitution which would protect human rights, curtail the madness which drives us, and allow the majority to affect changes leading to the above "normalcy".* (19)

[80] *Managed hostility is already underway. Developing a satisfactory narrative for the future of the settlements is the task of Israel's politicians and thinkers. The international community would be wise to encourage them in that task, rather than simply condemning the settlements out of hand.* (46)

[81] *Need for grassroots movements for peace. Take it to the streets and out of the hands of the leaders.* (13)

(25) were in favour of some form of a negotiated Two-State Solution. A third group (6%) preferred a One Shared State solution (3 respondents). A fourth group of 4 respondents (8%) did not have a specific solution. Particular differences emerged between the participants over their willingness to negotiate before a Palestinian renunciation of violence, and over the status of Jerusalem.

Rather than analyse further the specific points of disagreement which at present prevent an intra-group discourse from forming, it is possible to identify several competing discourses, which can be mapped on Ramsbotham's grid. For example, 'moderates' are willing to use the language of a secular-democratic one–state solution, compensation for refugees and settlements, significant cultural shifts to normalise the role of Israelo-Palestine in the region, and contemplate a pluralistic society where equal rights are given to all.[82] The majority discourse is of varieties of a two-state solution, with appropriate caveats over security, renunciation of violence, recognition of Israel, the problem of Jerusalem, etc. A third group, the "extremes" of the sample, hold to a simple one-state solution with the annexation of the territories, very limited autonomy for the Palestinians, and refusal to compromise or concede on territory.[83] With such internal dilemmas unaddressed, it is challenging to see how an intra-group Messianic Jewish discourse will emerge, but emerge it must, and the opportunity at this conference to engage with the 'moderate' and 'extreme' discourses of the other side provides a useful, if somewhat unpredictable, catalyst.

4. What do you think Messianic Jews can contribute to reconciliation and peace in the Arab-Israeli conflict? How can they do this?

a. No special contribution[84]

b. Special contribution of Messianic Jews[85]

---

[82] Respondents nos. 1, 8, 26, 33.

[83] Respondents nos. 18, 34, 39, 46.

[84] *On the human level, I believe we can do nothing meaningful. We're too small, too far from the consensus, and by far overly committed to a nationalistic stance (as a means of self-validation in the eyes of the Israeli Jewish public).* (21)
MJs have nothing unique to offer. They can join existing power structures that fit the individual's choice. (34)
It's hard to see what non-Israeli MJs could do. 'Like one who seizes a dog by the ears is a passer-by who meddles in a quarrel not his own.' (46)

[85] *All Christians can model Yeshua-like behaviour and be a witness for 'reconciliation'. They can pray continually 'for the peace of Jerusalem', support cross-group ministries like Musalaha ... MJs or Jewish Believers, specifically, are a sub-group of the above, and in a special position - We have a Jewish and a Christian (Yeshua-centred) perspective, despite our heterogeneity as a group. I think we need to be 'A light unto the Nations' still, and lead the way in reconciliation between Jews and Muslims in and around 'The Land'.* (1)

c. Prayer[86]

d. Preach the Gospel[87]

e. Reconciliation[88]

f. Fellowship and unity with Palestinian Christians[89]

g. Advocate for Israel[90]

h. Provide hope[91]

Messianic Jews should lead the way in being ambassadors of reconciliation. It is part of our very message in Yeshua! MJ's in the Land understand forgiveness, humility, the universal nature of Messiah's atonement, and God's future plan for Jew and Arab together in the Lord, so they should be reaching out to Arab leaders and others as much as possible to bridge the gap, even holding joint worship and prayer services -- hopefully, with strong media attention -- in order to be a witness to the nation. (7)

Messianic Jews lend a unique lens to the conflict, as they represent a Jewish perspective that must co-inhere with the message and mission of Yeshua. Messianic Jews' ability to fully experience the bond between the Jewish people and the land and to be deeply challenged by Yeshua's message of reconciliation and justice ought to translate into both an active interest and a unique perspective on the conflict. I am particularly hopeful about partnerships between Messianic Jews and Arab Christians, though Messianic Jewish engagement should not be limited to this alone. (33)

[86] *Messianic Jews can pray for the Israeli government to stand strong, with a strong resolve for truth. MJ's can also pray for our enemies that they would realize that they are fighting against the Almighty's plans for the restoration of the Jewish people to our homeland.* (41)

[87] *More prayer between the community of believers, more effective evangelism among Israelis and Arabs.* (47)

The body on both sides needs to focus on one thing and that is preaching the Gospel. They need to do this by being bold and loud. (35)

Evangelise everyone in the region because I have noted that Jews and Arabs that believe in Jesus can live in peace. (42)

[88] *Pray? Do our thing: fellowship with Palestinian brothers in the Lord in love and peace - not presuming that this will amount to solve the problems of the Middle East, but simply something good and beautiful.* (15)

Compassion for one's enemy is equally difficult to strive for outside of a long process of reconciliation. (40)

Israeli Messianic Jews can facilitate local efforts towards reconciliation and peace, for example by developing ways for Israeli Jews and Israeli Arabs to co-operate. (46)

[89] *Israeli MJs and Christian Arabs have a biblical duty to acknowledge and express their oneness in Messiah. (46)*

[90] *Of this, I'm unsure. I believe--like all Jews--we need to be ready (and well-prepared) to counter the usual Palestinian talking points that most people have swallowed because they are unaware of anything else, and be able to make a just and viable defence of Israel as a just, democratic (though imperfect) nation state.* (10)

[91] *Keep our people strong and hopeful. Raise awareness of injustice and inequality within our own society.* (13)

i. Challenge discourses of power[92]

j. Fighting injustice[93]

Reflection. 7% (3) saw no special contribution to be made by Messianic Jews, and the involvement of non-Israeli Messianic Jews as unhelpful. However, the majority saw a special contribution to be made by Messianic Jews, as a voice from the margins, as a prophetic sign and witness, and as a pioneering means of reconciliation between Israelis and Palestinians. They represent a Jewish perspective on belief in Yeshua which must conform to his own message and ministry. They have a responsibility to pray, preach and live out the Gospel, and demonstrate their unity in the Body of Christ with their Palestinian brothers and sisters. They are also called to advocate for Israel, whilst calling Israel to hope, justice and (for some) willingness to make hard choices and compromises. A small number believed Messianic Jews should take a more active role in advocacy, campaigning and political engagement. Most did not. The majority voiced the same arguments and positions found in Israeli political discourse.[94] No respondent discussed relations to Christian Zionism.

My hope is that the younger generation will finally become weary of the stagnation in the political sphere and ongoing conflict on the ground and will learn to truly listen to the other side in the conflict. In the current international climate there is an increasing focus on human rights issues and many in both the Arab and Jewish sectors are impacted by this focus. Peace, however, needs to be clearly defined and a definition mutually agreed before there is any long-term resolution to the conflict. (20)
I always have hope, but I am not sure about peace, but a cessation of hostilities, perhaps. (47)

[92] *Being marginal in numbers their role is not in forming lobbies or in political manoeuvring but in "speaking evangelically" and "thinking prophetically". Speaking evangelically means speaking about the situation and all the parties in the situation as Jesus would - loving and expressing that love. Thinking prophetically means opening up creative options that may not be part of current thinking. Political discourse here is ultimately very impoverished: two states, one state ... Coming from the margins, we should have the freedom to think the situation in new ways, ways that are not colonized by discourses of power, success and probability.* (26)

[93] *The Messianic community must unflinchingly stand for and declare openly the truth of the Gospel both in its spiritual application to our people/s and also in its moral imperatives. This would include calling our own government to account for the three major injustices for which we have been twice cast into the galut; the sins of the Canaanites, the injustices to the needy and helpless, and the shedding of innocent blood. We must also reach out in love and support to those who are brothers in Messiah, Jew, Arab, Israeli or Palestinian. If we do not, we as believers in the Land will be judged in kind!* (19)
Fighting against injustice against Palestinians in Israel e.g. over land confiscation. (28)

[94] Daniel Bar-Tal, *Ethos of Conflict*, 99, identifies the following societal beliefs that make up the 'ethos of conflict' which affect Israeli perceptions: the justness of the goals of Zionism to return to the Land and re-establish a State; the importance of security; a positive collective self-image of heroism and moral self-respect; self-perception as victims; delegitimization and dehumanization of the adversary, blaming them for instigation of the conflict and reluctance to find a solution; patriotism and willingness to identify and make sacrifices for the group; disregard of internal conflict to unite against external threat; portraying peace as most ardent wish despite the ongoing conflict.

Several observations can be made from the findings of this short, general but hopefully representative survey, which are of significance as we consider how a Messianic Jewish discourse may strategically engage with the discourses of others. First, it is apparent that Messianic Jews are like others, highly opinionated on the conflict, and are not reluctant, judging from the high response rate, to express them.[95] Yet they have not found an appropriate public forum to put their views forward except in circles where they meet with acceptance. Messianic Jews do not have a visible political voice or platform in Israel, and their discourse is often indistinguishable from the larger Jewish and Christian communities within which they belong.[96] See table 2 (below) for a comparison of Messianic Jewish and Israeli positions.

	Jewish Sovereignty	**Jewish Identity**	**MJ Views**	**MJ reconciliation role**
A Jewish Home	Nation-state (territory)	Religious Orthodox Zionist militaristic hegemony	Dispensationalist eschatology - no compromise on territory[97]	No role
Two Homes for Two Peoples	Nation-state (people)	Secular Zionist statist hegemony	Recognition of pragmatic and ethical issues - attempt negotiated settlement	Limited role, personal reconciliation between Messianic Jews and Palestinian Christians
One Home for Two Peoples	None	Communal (Jewish in private & public sphere but not state)	Minority position - secular democratic model	Re-visioning of relationships of Israeli and Palestinians
A Shared Home	Limited Sovereignty	An ethnic territorial group (Jewishness = cultural autonomy)	Very minority position - yet to be explored	Yet to be explored

Table 2: Messianic Jewish positions compared with Oxford Research Group Israeli track

[95] Some (respondents nos. 13, 34) questioned the agenda behind the questionnaire and the researcher's own position, but still gave their responses. Respondents were given two weeks to respond, and sent one reminder.

[96] *I'm not sure what goes on among our congregations may be graced with the honorific title of "discussion". I know of none such. Israel's claims are taken for granted, often the more extreme claims, without any investigation of them or discussion of them. No consideration is given to Palestinian claims.* (21).

[97] For a more nuanced discussion on the relationship between Dispensationalism and present day realities than is possible here see Judith Mendelsohn Rood and Paul W. Rood, "Is Christian Zionism Based On Bad Theology?" in *Cultural Encounters: A Journal For The Theology Of Culture* (Volume 7, Number 1, 2011), 41-52.

Secondly, the variety of views they express show a heterogeneity of political, eschatological and psycho-social discourses, with little mutual engagement with one another, or joined-up thinking to express clear political theologies. There is as yet no forum for organised discussion on these topics. The clearest theological message to be heard is that of a strong eschatological hope linked to a profound pessimism on any human peace process. Other voices call for a reconciliation agenda, but this is not developed into a clear plan. The majority express a guarded pessimism, lacking in hope for the immediate future, dubious of any long-term outcome apart from the Second Coming of Christ.

To this writer the general lack of hope represents not only a failure to grasp the nature of the Good News of the Messiah in all its totality, but also cripples the ability of Messianic Jews to make a positive contribution or have something positive to say about the resolution of the conflict in which they are called to be peace-makers.[98] Without a strong theology of hope there can be not a positive engagement with the intractable nature of the Israeli-Palestinian conflict, and little motivation for involvement in it.

The need for joined-up theological thinking raises key issues about the hermeneutics and theological interpretation of the ongoing election of Israel, the continuation of the Land promises, the meaning of justice, peace and reconciliation in the light of the ongoing conflict, and the calling of Messianic Jews which are beyond the purpose of this study. Thes need focused attention by Messianic Jews if they are to present a community-based theology and practice of reconciliation. This has yet to be attempted. But it should be noted that the majority of respondents, but not all, did not share a common Christian Zionist position of refusal to compromise at all on negotiation of territory.[99]

Where the respondents did talk of reconciliation, this was fairly narrowly defined as between individual Messianic Jews and Palestinian Christians, without exploring the economic, social and political dimensions of reconciliation, or the issues of conflict resolution and just and sustainable peace. Only a few saw this as an important dimension of reconciliation.[100] The majority had not yet envisioned what might be involved in building an infra-

---

[98] Eleven respondents used the word 'hope'.

[99] *I do not believe in the 'unquestionable' right of Jews to own any part of the Land, including Jerusalem (which belongs to God). I think the end times and other Biblical material is mysterious and unlike the Gospel - which is clearer and advocates that God is Love and Love thy Neighbour etc. However I am a Zionist. I believe in a Jewish homeland, with respect and rights for the Alien amongst us. (1)*

[100] *This would include calling our own government to account for the three major injustices for which we have been twice cast into the galut* [exile]*; the sins of the Canaanites, the injustices to the needy and helpless, and the shedding of innocent blood. We must also reach out in love and support to those who are brothers in Messiah, Jew, Arab, Israeli or Palestinian. If we do not, we as believers in the Land will be judged in kind!* (19)

structure for peace-making within the Messianic Jewish community.[101] The majority appeared not to have experienced training or preparation for peace-making of the type provided by Musalaha, Caritas, etc.[102] The majority also reacted strongly to the "agonistic discourse" of some Palestinians and their advocates with an equally adversarial discourse. See table 3 (below) for Messianic Jewish views of politics, eschatology and reconciliation.

	MJ political view	MJ eschatology	MJ reconciliation involvement
One state solution	Right wing	Dispensationalist	None
Two State Solution	Moderate	Historical Premillennialist or Dispensationalist	Interpersonal
Secular democratic state	Left wing	Varies	Social transformation
Don't know/mind	Non-committed	Varies	Varies

Table 3: Messianic Jewish positions on political solutions, eschatology and reconciliation

7. Strategic Engagement of Messianic Jewish Discourse with Other Discourses

As we have seen, there is not yet a unified strategic Messianic Jewish discourse that is able to engage with other discourses, but the attempt should be made if Messianic Jews are to play any part in conflict resolution and reconciliation. Whilst my own personal position is to the left of most of those surveyed, my purpose is to encourage greater interdependence within the Messianic movement and the formation of a shared discourse on this and other subjects.[103] Therefore my comments on the engagement of Messianic Jewish discourse with the discourses of others I hope reflect a broad consensus within the Messianic movement. How does a Messianic Jewish theology engage within the conflict complexes we identified previously?

The first partners for engagement of discourse are the Palestinian Christians. Here we encounter a variety of positions. Some who are Christian Zionist in

---

[101] Lederach, *Building Peace,* 73-85.

[102] Salim Munayer (ed.), *Musalaha: A Curriculum of Reconciliation* (Musalaha Ministry of Reconciliation: Jerusalem, 2011); Caritas International (Reina Neufeldt, Larissa Fast, Fr. Robert Schreiter, Fr. Brian Starken, Duncan MacLaren, Jaco Cilliers, John Paul Lederach), *Peacebuilding: A Caritas Training Manual* (Rome: Vatican City, 2002, 2006), http://www.caritas.org.

[103] This is the method and approach I adopt for the study and development of Messianic Jewish Theology in general. See Harvey, *Mapping Messianic Jewish Theology,* 277-279.

their strong support, others who are "apolitical", and others engaged as theological and political activists promoting Palestinian Liberation Theological Perspectives.[104] Messianic Jews need to address personally, politically and theologically their concerns. We need to develop our personal friendships and serious engagement with one another at every level as individuals, congregations and societies. My questions to my Palestinian Christian brothers and sisters, which may be taken up in discussion, are: who is willing to sit down with me, a Messianic Jew, to discuss these matters, and where do we start? How do we distinguish between the agonistic discourses that delegitimise and alienate us from one another, from the strategic engagement of discourses that will allow us to formulate options together? How will we learn to make painful compromises together? How will we deal together with issues of truth, mercy, justice and peace?[105]

The second partners in discourse are those in the wider Church. This includes both Arab Christians, Anti-Christian Zionists (those who oppose Christian Zionism) and Christian Anti-Zionists (those Christians who oppose Israeli/Jewish Zionism). Messianic Jews need to engage with supersessionist theology and anti-Judaism in Christian theology. We need to engage with Palestinian Liberation Theology and it own hermeneutic of Scripture, which Messianic Jews see as an extreme example of spiritualising and universalising the particularity of the election of Israel. We also need to engage with the adversarial discourse of Christian advocates and activists who take an "extreme" position. We need to engage with Christian Zionists whose hermeneutical approach and political agenda, as this conference has sought to challenge, needs refocusing on a biblical and ethical Zionism that includes God's purposes for all nations.

If possible "moderate" Messianic Jews should find partners who are also "moderate" so that an intergroup discourse can emerge between those on both sides. There is a particular challenge as "extreme" positions feed off each other to perpetuate the conflict. Christian Zionists and Anti-Christian Zionists contribute to the "extreme" of the inter-group discourse. Messianic Jews may be able to play a mediating role between these two groups, but will be viewed with suspicion by both. But Messianic Jews are in a position to challenge both "extremes", and to produce new possibilities for discourse and action. As Ramsbotham states:

> It is true that in the furnace of intense political conflict, variety is melted down into bipolar confrontations that generate radical disagreement, a

---

[104] See Yohanna Katanacho, "Palestinian Protestant Theological Responses to a World Marked by Violence" in *Missiology: An International Review,* Vol. XXXVI, no. 3, (July 2008), 289-305.

[105] Substantive proposals will need to be made and presented as a result of the intra-group discourse of both sides so that they can engage with the other party. This paper goes some way to preparing for this, and will be further developed.

process much studied in the analysis of conflict polarization and conflict escalation. But enquiry into the resultant radical disagreements equally regularly uncovers a persistent generation of new and ever-varying discrepancies. And these offer a starting point - even in the most intransigent phases of the conflict – for possible future reconfigurations and realignments.[106]

Messianic Jewish discourse, with its particular perspectives and sensitivities, may well produce new options for engagement between the parties and contribute to the leverage necessary to bring great traction to the intractability of the Israeli-Palestinian conflict.

The third level of engagement is with our own people. A coherent Messianic Jewish discourse has yet to emerge within Israel and the Jewish people, as we are still very much on the margins of political and social space. My prayer is for this to develop as Messianic Jews become more visible and accepted. Our purpose as Jewish believers in the Messiah of Israel is to speak out and live out his message of reconciliation, between us and God, and between all humanity.

8. Concluding Proposals

The modest proposals that conclude this paper are that Messianic Jews need to formulate their own intra-group discourse and then engage with the discourses of others. They need to develop a Theology and Praxis of Reconciliation on the basis of a conjectural analysis of context, resources and what needs to be done.[107] They need to respond to the call to be peacemakers through familiarisation, training, equipping and engagement in the process of reconciliation.

The asymetries of power in the different conflict systems mean that the Messianic movement is already a group on the margins of mainstream Israeli, Jewish and Christian discourse, with little (amongst Christian Zionists) or no (amongst Mainstream Israeli) influence. Whether we will have influence among Palestinian Christians, Anti-Christian Zionists and Christian Anti-Zionists remains to be seen, but I personally am hopeful that interactions such as this will be fruitful in clarifying the agenda for discussions and removing some of the stereotypes and misconceptions.

Messianic Jews, as the "remnant saved by grace", are the "missing link" that unites the Church and Israel. They are called to be a powerful prophetic

---

[106] Ramsbotham, 18.

[107] Lederach, *Building Peace,* 119. "The capacity to identify, understand and strategically analyze the immediate situation-in-context, with an eye toward locating the social, political and economic and cultural relationships that may block and/or hold potential for creative transformation of conflicts."

symbol of God's ongoing election of Israel, his faithfulness to his promises, and his saving purposes for all nations. They are also called to walk the path of reconciliation, both in the process, product and character of life that embodies Yeshua's reconciling love to all humanity and to all creation.

The road to reconciliation is not easy:

> Reconciliation is probably the most difficult condition because it asks for a deep cognitive change, a real change of beliefs, ideology, and emotions not only among the ruling elites but also among most if not all sectors of both societies.[108]

It must overcome the roadblocks of:

> Conflicting perceptions, embattled beliefs, hardened attitudes, opposed truths, segmented realities, contrasting mental worlds, antithetic ideological axioms, incompatible ideological beliefs, alternative mental representations, differing views about reality, divergent discursive representations, different discourse worlds. [109]

To do so Messianic Jews must build a peace-making infrastructure within their own communities and theologies that may build bridges to those of others. Lederach describes this as

> the set of capacities and linkages and the web of relationships needed to sustain a peace process. [110]

Caritas notes that

> an infrastructure is needed to provide the social spaces, logistical mechanisms, and institutions necessary for supporting the process of change and long-term vision of peace.[111]

Most of all, Messianic Jews need a theology and ethic of hope.[112] Without hope there exists little motivation for a theology and practise of reconciliation. One survey respondent commented:

---

[108] Bar-Siman-Tov, *From Conflict Resolution to Reconciliation*, 4.
[109] Ramsbotham, 7.
[110] Howard Clark, "Campaigning Power and Civil Courage: Bringing 'People Power' back into Conflict Transformation" in *Committee for Conflict Transformation Support Review* (no. 27), May 2005, 4.
[111] Caritas 2006:197, adapted from Lederach, 1997.
[112] I am thinking of a Messianic Jewish equivalent of Jürgen Moltmann's *Theology of Hope* (London: SCM Press, 1974) which attempts to ground eschatological hope in present social and political reality through the cross and resurrection of Christ. See also Jürgen Moltmann, *Ethics of Hope*. London, SCM Press, 2012.

> The idea of a Messianic Theology on Reconciliation is almost absurd, the movement is diverse and this is a topic that to my knowledge has never been broached or discussed.[113]

This paper has only made modest steps towards the construction of a Theology of Reconciliation, by setting in contexts and surveying the prospects for an intra-group discourse amongst Messianic Jews which will allow them to formulate strategic options that can then engage with the discourses of others. We have not examined the key theological rationale or themes within the theology of reconciliation, nor urged a particular program of action. But if this paper could add one consideration to the forming of a MJTOR, it would be the need for hope.

I am here at this conference not to propose solutions or critique the views of others so much as to call for the process and product or reconciliation, between Messianic Jew and Palestinian Christian, and ultimately between Jew and Arab, and all humanity, in a redeemed and restored creation. I have come here to listen, to learn, to talk together and pray together, and thank you for this opportunity to be here. I ask for your help and prayers to see my people come to know the Saviour we have in common, and to live out his message of reconciliation. Thank you.

9. Bibliography

Auerbach, Yehudith. "The Role of Forgiveness in Reconciliation". In Yaacov Bar-Siman-Tov, *From Conflict Resolution to Reconciliation,* 149-175. Oxford, OUP, 2004.

Bar-Siman-Tov, Yaacov (ed.). *From Conflict Resolution to Reconciliation.* Oxford: OUP, 2004.

Bar-Tal, Daniel, Amiram Raviv, Alona Raviv and Adi Dgani-Hirsh. "The Influence of the Ethos of Conflict on Israeli Jews' Interpretation of Jewish–Palestinian Encounters". *Journal of Conflict Resolution* (Volume 53 Number 1, February 2009), 94-118. http://tau.ac.il/~daniel/pdf/31.pdf.

Bar-Tal, Daniel, and Gemma H. Bennink. "The nature of reconciliation as an outcome and as a process". In Yaacov Bar-Siman- Tov (ed.). *From Conflict Resolution to Reconciliation* (pp.11-38). Oxford: Oxford University Press (also published in Politika, 2002, Issue No 9, pp. 9-34 in Hebrew).

---

[113] *The idea of a Messianic Theology on Reconciliation is almost absurd, the movement is diverse and this is a topic that to my knowledge has never been broached or discussed. Also the Theology of Messianic Judaism in Israel should be significantly different.*
2. Your questions reflect [either] a bias or a leading. The presupposition is that there is something Israel must do.
3. The presumption that our individual opinion matters whereas the direction of our communities lies at the heart of the issue. (Respondent 13)

Bröning, Michael. *The Politics of Change in Palestine: State-Building and Non-Violent Resistance.* London: Pluto Press, 2011.

Chaitim, J. "Bridging the Impossible? Confronting Barriers to Dialogue between Israelis and Germans and Between Israelis and Palestinians". *International Journal of Peace Studies,* 13 (2): 33-58.

Clark, Howard. "Campaigning Power and Civil Courage: Bringing 'People Power' back into Conflict Transformation". *Committee for Conflict Transformation Support Review* (no. 27), May 2005, 4. http://www.c-r.org/ccts/ccts27/review27.pdf

Caritas International (Reina Neufeldt, Larissa Fast, Fr. Robert Schreiter, Fr. Brian Starken, Duncan MacLaren, Jaco Cilliers, John Paul Lederach). *Peacebuilding: A Caritas Training Manual.* Rome: Vatican City, 2002, 2006. http://www.caritas.org

Murray Silberling, "Messianic Judaism's Role in the Diaspora" pp. 185-192

and David Stern, "Messianic Jews Should Make Aliyah" in
Cohn-Sherbok, Dan (ed.). *Voices of Messianic Judaism: Confronting Critical Issues Facing a Maturing Movement.* Baltimore: Lederer Books, 2001.,; 193-202.

Constantineu, Corneliu. "Reconciliation as a Missiological Category for Social Engagement." In *Bible and Mission: A Conversation between Biblical Studies and Missiology.* An Occasional Publication of the International Baptist Theological Seminary. IBTS: Czech Republic. Germany; Neufeld Verlag 2008. 132-159.

Cordell, Karl and Stefan Wolff (eds.). *Routledge Handbook of Ethnic Conflict.*

Dijk, Teun A. van . "What is political discourse analysis?" Key-note address, Congress Political Linguistics. Antwerp, 7-9 -December 1995. In Jan Blommaert and Chris Bulcaen (eds.), *Political Linguistics* (Amsterdam: Benjamins, 1997), 11-52.

Gans, Chaim. *A Just Zionism: On the Morality of the Jewish State.* Oxford: OUP, 2008.

Gruchy, John de. *Reconciliation: Restoring Justice.* London: SCM Press, 2002.

Harvey, Richard S. "Implicit 'Universalism' in Some Christian Zionism and Messianic Judaism". In *Jesus, Salvation and the Jewish People: The Uniqueness of Jesus and Jewish Evangelism.* David Parker (ed.). UK: Paternoster, 2011.

————————. *Mapping Messianic Jewish Theology: A Constructive Approach.* Carlisle: Paternoster/Authentic Media, 2010.

———————— "The Need for a Bridging Narrative". In Concordis International. *British Churches and the Israeli-Palestinian Conflict.* Concordis Papers VIII. Cambridge: Concordis International, 2010, pp. 10-11.

————————. "Towards a Messianic Jewish Theology of Reconciliation in the Light of the Arab-Israeli Conflict: Neither Dispensationalist nor Supersessionist?" In *The Land Cries Out: Theology of the Land in the Israeli-Palestinian Context.* Salim J. Munayer and Lisa Loden (eds.), USA: Cascade/Wipf and Stock, 2011.

——————— "What Shapes Jewish Identity?" *Sixth International Conference 1999 Conference Booklet*. Kai Kjær-Hansen and Bødil Skjott, eds. Lausanne Consultation on Jewish Evangelism, August 13, 1999), 72-85.

Ho, Iris. "A critical evaluation of Christian approaches to the Israeli-Palestinian conflict". Research Paper, All Nations Christian College, 2010.

Houston, Judy. "Towards Interdependence, Remembrance and Justice: Reconciliation Ministry in the Israeli/Palestinian Context". MA Dissertation, All Nations Christian College, 2006.

Jeon, Ho-Won. *Conflict Management and Resolution: An Introduction*. Routledge, 2009.

Just Vision. *Encounter Point.* Brooklyn, NY . www.justvision.org. no date.

Katanacho, Yohanna. "Palestinian Protestant Theological Responses to a World Marked by Violence." In *Missiology: An International Review,* Vol. XXXVI, no. 3, (July 2008), 289-305.

Kjær-Hansen, Kai (ed.). *Israel, the Land, and Christian Zionism*. Articles in *Mishkan,* UCCI/Caspari Centre: Jerusalem, 2008.

Lausanne Committee for World Evnagelization. *Reconciliation as the Mission of God: Faithful Christian Witness in a World of Destructive Conflicts and Divisions*. Lausanne Occasional Papers no. 51. Pattaya, Thailand, 2004. Available online at http://www.lausanne.org/en/documents/lops/867-lop-51.html.

Lederach, J. *Building Peace – Sustainable Reconciliation in Divided Societies.* Tokyo: United Nations University Press, 1997.

Loden, Lisa, Peter Walker, and Michael Wood. *The Bible and the Land: An Encounter*. Jerusalem: Musalaha, 2000.

Loden, Lisa and Salim Munayer. *The Land Cries Out: Theology of the Land in the Israeli-Palestinian Context.* Oregon: Cascade/Wipf and Stock, 2011.

Maiese, Michelle. "Peacebuilding" in *Beyond Intractability*. Ed. Guy Burgess and Heidi Burgess, Conflict Information Consortium, University of Colorado, Boulder, Colorado, USA, 2005.
<http://www.beyondintractability.org/bi-essay/development-conflict-theory>.
http://www.beyondintractability.org/print/2714

Maoz, Baruch. "The Christian Embassy in Jerusalem". In *Mishkan* (Issue 12) on "Christian Zionism". UCCI/Caspari Centre, Jerusalem, 1990.

Merkely, Paul Charles. *Christian Attitudes Towards the State of Israel.* USA: McGill-Queen's University Press, 2001.

Moltmann, Jürgen. *Theology of Hope.* London, SCM Press, 1969.

Moltmann, Jürgen. *Ethics of Hope.* London, SCM Press, 2012.

Munayer, Salim (ed.) *Musalaha: A Curriculum of Reconciliation*. Musalaha Ministry of Reconciliation: Jerusalem, 2011.

Pan, Nancy. "How and to what extend can an expatriate worker participate and contribute to a model and process of discipleship, which focuses on reconciliation in the context of the Israeli/Palestinian conflict?" Research Paper, All Nations Christian College, 2011.

Ramsbotham, Oliver. "Radical Disagreement and Systemic Conflict Transformation" in *The Non-Linearity of Peace Processes – Theory and Practice of Systemic Conflict Transformation.* D. Körppen, N. Ropers and Hans J. Gießmann (eds.). Opladen/Farmington Hills: Barbara Budrich Verlag, 2011.
berghof-peacesupport.org/books/sct_book_2011_Ramsbotham.pdf

Ramsbotham, Oliver. *Transforming Violent Conflict: Radical Disagreement, Dialogue and Survival.* London and New York: Routledge, 2010.

Rey, Cheryl de la. "Reconciliation in Divided Societies." In Christie, D. J., R.V. Wagner and D.A. Winter (eds.). *Peace, Conflict, and Violence: Peace Psychology for the 21st Century.* Englewood Cliffs, New Jersey: Prentice-Hall, 2001. Available online at http://academic.marion.ohio-state.edu/dchristie/Peace%20Psychology%20Book_files/Chapter%2021%20-%20Reconciliation%20in%20Divided%20Societies%20%28de%20la%20Rey%29.pdf

Riggans, Walter. "The Messianic Jewish Community and the Handshake," *Anvil* 11.2 (1994): 145-156.

Rood, Judith Mendelsohn and Paul W. Rood. "Is Christian Zionism Based On Bad Theology?" *Cultural Encounters: A Journal For The Theology Of Culture* . Volume 7, Number 1, 2011, 41-52.

Rotberg, Robert L. (ed.) *Israeli and Palestinian Narratives of Conflict: History's Double Helix.* Bloomington: Indiana University Press, 2006.

Sadan, Tsvi. "Christ at the Checkpoint - and Now the Movie". In *Kivun* 71, Jerusalem, June-July 2010, pp. 17-18 (Hebrew).

Sadan, Tsvi. "The Land He has given to the children of men – except the Zionists". In *Kivun* 70, April-May 2010, pp. 7-8.

Schreiter, Robert J. "Reconciliation and Peacemaking: The Theology of Reconciliation and Peacemaking for Mission". In *Mission, Violence and Reconciliation.* Eds. Howard Mellor and Timothy Yates. Sheffield: Cliff College Publishing, 2004.

Schreiter, Robert J. *The Ministry of Reconciliation: Spirituality and Strategies.* Maryknoll: Orbis, 1998.

Schwöbel, Christoph. "Reconciliation: From Biblical Observations to Dogmatic Reconstruction." In *The Theology of Reconciliation*, ed. Colin E. Gunton, 13-38. London: T. & T. Clark, 2003.

Silberling, Murray. "Messianic Judaism's Role in the Diaspora". In Dan Cohn-Sherbok (ed.), *Voices of Messianic Judaism: Confronting Critical Issues Facing a Maturing Movement.* Baltimore: Lederer Books, 2001, pp. 193-202.

Skjøtt, Bodil. 'Messianic Believers and the Land of Israel – a Survey.' Mishkan 26, no. 1 (1997): 72-81.

Soulen, R. Kendall. *The God of Israel and Christian Theology.* Minneapolis: Fortress Press, 1999.

Stern, David. "Messianic Jews Should Make Aliyah". In Dan Cohn-Sherbok (ed.), *Voices of Messianic Judaism: Confronting Critical Issues Facing a Maturing Movement.* Baltimore: Lederer Books, 2001, pp. 185-192

Walker, Peter W. L. (ed.). *Jerusalem Past and Present in the Purposes of God.* Cambridge: Tyndale House, 1992, 2nd rev. ed. 1994.

Wallenstein, Peter. *Understanding Conflict Resolution: War, Peace and the Global System.* 3rd ed., London: Sage Publications, 2011.

Ware, Helen (ed.). *The No-Nonsense Guide to Conflict and Peace.* UK: New Internationalist Publications, 2006, 2007.

Wright, Christopher J. H. *The Mission of God: Unlocking the Bible's Grand Narrative.* Downers Wood: IVP, 2006.

Zalzberg, Ofer. *EU Partnership For Peace – Israeli Track* . Oxford Research Group Jerusalem, 22 April 2009.

Zayyad, Ziad Abu and Hillel Schenker, eds. "Palestinian Refugees and the Two-State Solution: Findings and recommendations of an expert roundtable discussion." Palestine-Israel Journal, PIJ Policy Paper No. 3. Jerusalem, December 2009. http://www.pij.org/pijpapers/refugees_pijpaper.pdf

www.ingramcontent.com/pod-product-compliance
Ingram Content Group UK Ltd.
Pitfield, Milton Keynes, MK11 3LW, UK
UKHW020228250726
13967UKWH00001B/257